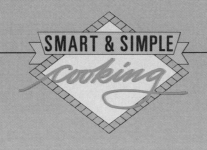

SMART & SIMPLE

cooking

Microwave Notes

The 15-MINUTES or Less Microwave cookbook has been specially designed to meet your need for fast, tasty food that is easy to prepare. Each recipe has a cooking time of no longer than 15 minutes.

It is important to note that these recipes were tested on a 650-watt microwave oven. The settings ranging from LOW to HIGH are derived from this wattage, with HIGH being 100% of our oven's power. Because microwave ovens differ, consult your manufacturer's booklet for setting and/or time changes that may be necessary.

Aside from the frequently used microwave-safe utensils, you will also need a "browning grill," which has been used in a selection of meat recipes. A special coating on the underside of the grill absorbs microwave energy during preheating, causing the surface to become very hot. When the food is added it immediately begins to sear and the end result after microwaving is much what you would expect from skillet cooking. We have found this tool to be invaluable and are quite certain that you will too. Please be sure to read the manufacturer's instruction booklet for this utensil and adjust preheating times if necessary.

Until we cook again...

Cheese Bites

(serves 4-6)

1 SERVING	326 CALORIES	15g CARBOHYDRATE
9g PROTEIN	26g FAT	0.1g FIBER

Setting: HIGH

Cooking time: 1½ minutes

Utensil: microwave trivet

1 cup	(250 ml) grated cheddar cheese
½ cup	(125 ml) mayonnaise
3 tbsp	(45 ml) chopped chives
¼ cup	(50 ml) grated Gruyère cheese
6	pitted black olives, chopped
¼ tsp	(1 ml) Tabasco sauce
	pepper
	assorted crackers or toasted rounds

Place all ingredients, except crackers, in food processor. Blend 4 minutes or until smooth.

Spread mixture over crackers, place on trivet and microwave 1½ minutes uncovered.

Serve as an appetizer.

Chick Pea Spread

(serves 4-6)

1 SERVING	148 CALORIES	24g CARBOHYDRATE
6g PROTEIN	3g FAT	4.4g FIBER

Setting: HIGH

Cooking time: 15 minutes

Utensil: 12 cup (3 L) casserole

1 tbsp	(15 ml) melted butter
3 tbsp	(45 ml) chopped onion
2	garlic cloves, smashed and chopped
19 oz	(540 ml) can chick peas, drained
1	potato, peeled and sliced paper thin
¼ tsp	(1 ml) coriander
¼ tsp	(1 ml) cinnamon
¼ tsp	(1 ml) chili powder
¼ tsp	(1 ml) sugar
2 tbsp	(30 ml) tomato paste
3 tbsp	(45 ml) tomato sauce
¼ tsp	(1 ml) Worcestershire sauce
3 tbsp	(45 ml) sour cream

Place butter, onion, garlic, chick peas, potato, seasonings and sugar in casserole. Mix very well and cover with plastic wrap; microwave 10 minutes.

Mix well and stir in tomato paste; continue microwaving 5 minutes, covered.

Transfer to food processor and blend until smooth.

Add tomato sauce, Worcestershire sauce and sour cream; blend again.

Place chick pea spread in bowl, cover and refrigerate until cold.

Serve with vegetables and/or crackers.

Tomato Garlic Bread

(serves 6-8)

1 SERVING	210 CALORIES	30g CARBOHYDRATE
9g PROTEIN	6g FAT	3.3g FIBER

Setting: HIGH
Cooking time: 8 minutes
Utensil: 12 cup (3 L) casserole

2	garlic cloves, smashed and chopped
1 tsp	(5 ml) olive oil
28 oz	(796 ml) can tomatoes, drained and chopped
4 tbsp	(60 ml) tomato paste
¼ tsp	(1 ml) sugar
1 cup	(250 ml) grated mozzarella cheese
	salt and pepper
	sliced Italian bread, toasted in conventional oven
	garlic butter

Place garlic, oil, tomatoes, tomato paste and sugar in casserole; season generously. Microwave 8 minutes uncovered, stirring once.

Spread garlic butter over toasted bread and cover with tomato mixture. Top with cheese and broil in conventional oven until melted.

Julienne of Vegetables Soup

(serves 4)

1 SERVING	88 CALORIES	14g CARBOHYDRATE
1g PROTEIN	3g FAT	1.7g FIBER

Setting: HIGH
Cooking time: 13 minutes
Utensil: 12 cup (3 L) casserole

1	carrot, pared
1	celery stalk
1	small zucchini
1	garlic clove, smashed and chopped
1	bay leaf
1 tbsp	(15 ml) butter
1 cup	(250 ml) cooked rice
3½ cups	(875 ml) hot chicken stock
	salt and pepper

Cut vegetables into fine julienne about 1 in (2.5 cm) long.

Place vegetables, garlic, bay leaf and butter in casserole. Cover and microwave 3 minutes.

Mix well, season and continue cooking another 4 minutes, covered.

Add remaining ingredients and microwave 6 minutes uncovered.

Correct seasoning and serve.

Asparagus Soup

(serves 2)

1 SERVING	260 CALORIES	17g CARBOHYDRATE
6g PROTEIN	19g FAT	1.6g FIBER

Setting: HIGH
Cooking time: 13 minutes
Utensil: 12 cup (3 L) casserole

2 tbsp	(30 ml) butter
1	bunch fresh asparagus, diced small
½	celery stalk, diced
2 tbsp	(30 ml) chopped onion
2½ tbsp	(40 ml) flour
1½ cups	(375 ml) hot milk
½ cup	(125 ml) light cream
¼ tsp	(1 ml) nutmeg
	salt and pepper
	dash paprika
	chicken stock (optional)

Place butter, asparagus, celery and onion in casserole; season well. Cover and microwave 7 minutes, stirring once during cooking process.

Mix in flour until well incorporated. Add remaining ingredients, mix well and let stand 2 minutes uncovered.

Season soup and finish microwaving 6 minutes uncovered.

Remove and purée in food processor. Reheat if necessary and serve.

If soup is too thick, dilute with chicken stock.

Potato and Pepper Soup

(serves 4)

1 SERVING	186 CALORIES	28g CARBOHYDRATE
7g PROTEIN	5g FAT	1.7g FIBER

Setting: HIGH

Cooking time: 15 minutes

Utensil: 12 cup (3 L) casserole

3 cups	(750 ml) hot chicken stock
4	potatoes, peeled and in julienne
1	green pepper, halved and sliced
5	mushrooms, sliced
¼ tsp	(1 ml) paprika
½ cup	(125 ml) grated Gruyère cheese

pinch nutmeg

pinch oregano

salt and pepper

Pour chicken stock into casserole and add potatoes. Microwave 10 minutes uncovered.

Add green pepper, mushrooms, paprika, salt and pepper; continue microwaving 5 minutes uncovered.

Sprinkle in cheese, nutmeg and oregano; mix and serve.

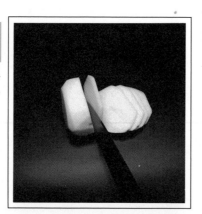
1 Square off peeled potatoes and slice lengthwise.

3 Microwave vegetables in hot chicken stock.

2 Cut into fine julienne.

4 Mix in cheese and seasonings and serve.

Spinach Parmentier

(serves 4)

1 SERVING	217 CALORIES	32g CARBOHYDRATE
6g PROTEIN	7g FAT	3.5g FIBER

Setting: HIGH

Cooking time: 15 minutes

Utensil: 12 cup (3 L) casserole

1 tbsp	(15 ml) butter
2 tbsp	(30 ml) chopped onion
1 tsp	(5 ml) sugar
4	potatoes, peeled and sliced
¼ tsp	(1 ml) thyme
½ tsp	(2 ml) sweet basil
2 cups	(500 ml) chopped cooked spinach
2½ cups	(625 ml) boiling chicken stock
½ cup	(125 ml) cold light cream
	salt and pepper
	dash anise

Place butter, onion, sugar, potatoes, thyme and sweet basil in casserole. Season well and add anise.

Cover with chopped spinach and pour in chicken stock. Cover and microwave 15 minutes.

Transfer contents to food processor; blend until puréed.

Pour soup into terrine, stir in cream and serve.

Chilled Curried Zucchini Soup

(serves 4)

1 SERVING	146 CALORIES	13g CARBOHYDRATE
3g PROTEIN	9g FAT	1.4g FIBER

Setting: HIGH

Cooking time: 14 minutes

Utensil: 12 cup (3 L) casserole

1 tbsp	(15) butter
1	celery stalk, sliced
6	mushrooms, sliced
1	zucchini, halved lengthwise and sliced
¼ tsp	(1 ml) ground ginger
1 ½ tbsp	(25 ml) curry powder
1 ½ tbsp	(25 ml) flour
10 oz	(284 ml) can condensed cream of mushroom soup
2 cups	(500 ml) hot water
	salt and pepper

Place butter, celery, mushrooms, zucchini, salt, pepper, ginger and curry in casserole. Cover and microwave 3 minutes.

Stir vegetables. Mix in flour until well incorporated.

Place condensed soup in bowl; whisk in water until well incorporated. Add to casserole, mix well and correct seasoning.

Microwave 11 minutes uncovered, stirring occasionally.

Pour soup into food processor and purée.

Refrigerate and serve cold.

Cold Curried Vegetable Soup

(serves 4)

1 SERVING	150 CALORIES	11g CARBOHYDRATE
2g PROTEIN	11g FAT	1.2g FIBER

Setting: HIGH

Cooking time: 15 minutes

Utensil: 12 cup (3 L) casserole

3 tbsp	(45 ml) butter
1	celery stalk, sliced
1	red onion, halved and sliced
1½ tbsp	(25 ml) curry powder
1 tsp	(5 ml) cumin
3 tbsp	(45 ml) flour
¼ tsp	(1 ml) paprika
½	zucchini, thinly sliced
½	green apple, thinly sliced
2½ cups	(625 ml) boiling chicken stock
4 tbsp	(60 ml) sour cream
	salt and pepper

Place butter, celery and onion in casserole; season well. Cover and microwave 2 minutes.

Sprinkle in curry and cumin; cover and microwave 2 minutes.

Mix well and stir in flour and paprika; mix again.

Add zucchini and apple. Pour in chicken stock, season and stir. Microwave 11 minutes uncovered, stirring every 3 minutes.

Transfer contents to food processor and blend until puréed.

Top servings with sour cream.

Place butter, celery and onion in casserole; season well. Cover and microwave 2 minutes.

Sprinkle in curry and cumin; cover and microwave 2 minutes.

Mix well and stir in flour and paprika; mix again.

Add zucchini and apple.

Shrimp Soup

(serves 4)

1 SERVING	224 CALORIES	7g CARBOHYDRATE
20g PROTEIN	13g FAT	0.1g FIBER

Setting: HIGH

Cooking time: 15 minutes

Utensil: 12 cup (3 L) casserole

3 tbsp	(45 ml) butter
½	small red onion, chopped
1 tbsp	(15 ml) chopped parsley
½ lb	(250 g) fresh frozen shrimp, thawed
3 tbsp	(45 ml) flour
½ cup	(125 ml) canned clams
½ cup	(125 ml) clam juice, heated
1½ cups	(375 ml) boiling light chicken stock
½ cup	(125 ml) light cream
	salt and pepper

Place butter, onion, parsley and shrimp in casserole. Season, cover and microwave 4 minutes.

Mix in flour until well incorporated.

Add clams and heated juice; mix well. Pour in hot chicken stock and correct seasoning. Microwave 11 minutes uncovered, stirring every 3 minutes.

Transfer contents to food processor and blend until puréed.

Stir in cream and serve with lemon slices if desired.

Place butter, onion, parsley and shrimp in casserole. Season, cover and microwave 4 minutes.

Mix in flour until well incorporated.

Add clams and heated juice; mix well. Pour in chicken stock and correct seasoning. Microwave 11 minutes uncovered, stirring every 3 minutes.

Transfer contents to food processor and blend until puréed.

Mushroom Soup

(serves 4)

1 SERVING	150 CALORIES	8g CARBOHYDRATE
3g PROTEIN	12g FAT	0.7g FIBER

Setting: HIGH
Cooking time: 15 minutes
Utensil: 12 cup (3 L) casserole

3 tbsp	(45 ml) butter
2	shallots, chopped
½ lb	(250 g) mushrooms, chopped
1 tsp	(5 ml) lemon juice
3 tbsp	(45 ml) flour
2 cups	(500 ml) hot chicken stock
¼ cup	(50 ml) hot milk
¼ tsp	(1 ml) celery seed
1 tbsp	(15 ml) finely chopped parsley
	salt and pepper

Place butter, shallots, mushrooms and lemon juice in casserole. Cover and microwave 3 minutes.

Stir and mix in flour until well incorporated.

Add chicken stock, milk and celery seed; season well. Mix and microwave 12 minutes uncovered, stirring every 3 minutes.

Transfer contents to food processor and blend 1 minute.

Pour soup into terrine and sprinkle with parsley. Serve with croutons if desired.

Cream of Leek Soup

(serves 4)

1 SERVING	162 CALORIES	14g CARBOHYDRATE
2g PROTEIN	11g FAT	1.2g FIBER

Setting: HIGH
Cooking time: 14 minutes
Utensil: 12 cup (3 L) casserole

3 tbsp	(45 ml) butter
2	leeks, white section only, thinly sliced
1	small onion, thinly sliced
¼ tsp	(1 ml) celery seed
3 tbsp	(45 ml) flour
2	tomatoes, peeled, cored and sliced
½ tsp	(2 ml) sugar
3 cups	(750 ml) hot chicken stock
¼ cup	(50 ml) light cream
	salt and pepper

Place butter, leeks, onion and celery seed in casserole. Cover and microwave 3 minutes.

Mix in flour until well incorporated.

Add tomatoes, mix and add sugar and chicken stock; season well. Microwave 10 minutes uncovered, stirring every 3 minutes.

Stir in cream and finish microwaving 1 minute uncovered.

Transfer contents to food processor and blend 1 minute.

Serve with crackers.

Cream of Carrot Soup

(serves 4)

1 SERVING	83 CALORIES	11g CARBOHYDRATE
1g PROTEIN	4g FAT	1.8g FIBER

Setting: HIGH
Cooking time: 15 minutes
Utensil: 12 cup (3 L) casserole

1 tbsp	(15 ml) butter
½	onion, thinly sliced
1	celery stalk, thinly sliced
2	large carrots, pared and sliced
1	green apple, cored, peeled and thinly sliced
½ tsp	(2 ml) chervil
1	mint leaf
2½ cups	(625 ml) boiling chicken stock
¼ cup	(50 ml) hot light cream
	juice ½ lemon
	salt and ground pepper

Place butter, onion and celery in casserole. Cover and microwave 3 minutes.

Add carrots, apple, chervil, mint leaf, chicken stock and lemon juice. Mix and season well. Microwave 12 minutes uncovered.

Using slotted spoon, transfer vegetables to food processor and blend until puréed.

Replace puréed vegetables in casserole containing liquid. Whisk well, stir in cream and serve soup with soda crackers.

Cream of Lettuce Soup

(serves 4)

1 SERVING	171 CALORIES	12g CARBOHYDRATE
2g PROTEIN	13g FAT	1.0g FIBER

Setting: HIGH

Cooking time: 13 minutes

Utensil: 12 cup (3 L) casserole

1 tbsp	(15 ml) butter
1	onion, thinly sliced
1	celery stalk, sliced
1 tbsp	(15 ml) chopped parsley
2-3	mint leaves
1-2	sprigs fresh savory
1	sprig fresh dill
2 tbsp	(30 ml) flour
1	small escarole lettuce, well cleaned and shredded
10 oz	(284 ml) can condensed cream of mushroom soup
2 cups	(500 ml) hot water
3 tbsp	(45 ml) heavy cream (optional)
	salt and pepper

Place butter, onion, celery, parsley, mint, savory and dill in casserole; cover and microwave 1 minute.

Mix in flour until well incorporated.

Add lettuce and season well.

Place condensed soup in bowl; whisk in hot water until well incorporated.

Add soup to casserole, mix well and microwave 12 minutes uncovered.

Pour soup into food processor and blend 2 minutes.

If desired, mix in cream before serving.

Place butter, onion, celery, parsley, mint, savory and dill in casserole; cover and microwave 1 minute.

After flour has been incorporated, add lettuce and season well.

Add diluted soup to casserole, mix well and microwave 12 minutes uncovered.

Pour soup into food processor and blend 2 minutes.

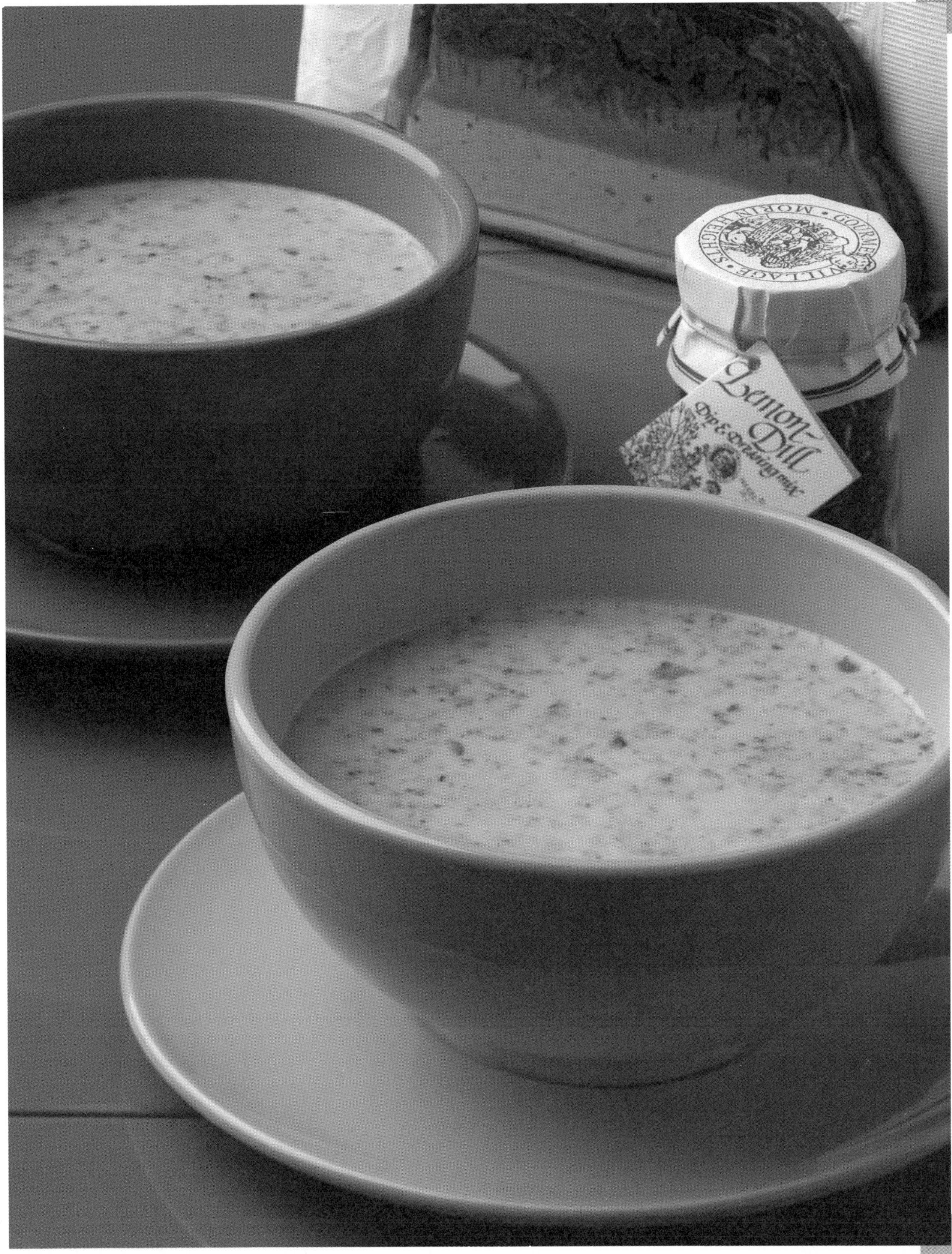
MORIN HEIGHTS • GOURMET VILLAGE
Lemon-Dill
Dip & Dressing mix

Stuffed Cabbage Rolls

(serves 2-3)

1 SERVING	226 CALORIES	28g CARBOHYDRATE
15g PROTEIN	6g FAT	2.9g FIBER

Setting: HIGH
Cooking time: 15 minutes
Utensil: 12 cup (3 L) casserole

1 cup	(250 ml) cooked rice
1	onion, chopped
½	green pepper, chopped
¼ tsp	(1 ml) Worcestershire sauce
1 tsp	(5 ml) soya sauce
¼ lb	(125 g) ground veal
2	garlic cloves, smashed and chopped
6	cabbage leaves, blanched
1 cup	(250 ml) tomato sauce
	few drops hot sauce
	salt and pepper

Place all ingredients, except cabbage and tomato sauce, in food processor; blend 3 minutes on high speed.

Blot cabbage leaves with paper towel to dry completely and lay flat on cutting surface. Spread stuffing over entire leaf and roll lengthwise.

Place stuffed cabbage rolls in casserole and pour in tomato sauce; season well.

Microwave 7 minutes uncovered.

Rotate casserole ½ turn; continue microwaving 8 minutes.

Onion Croustade

(serves 4)

1 SERVING	281 CALORIES	30g CARBOHYDRATE
11g PROTEIN	13g FAT	1.8g FIBER

Setting: HIGH and MEDIUM-HIGH
Cooking time: 13 minutes
Utensil: 12 cup (3 L) casserole

1½ tbsp	(25 ml) melted butter
5	onions, halved and thinly sliced
½ tsp	(2 ml) nutmeg
2½ tbsp	(40 ml) flour
1½ cups	(375 ml) hot milk
1 tbsp	(15 ml) curry powder
½ cup	(125 ml) grated cheddar cheese
	salt and pepper
	toasted French bread

Place butter, onions and plenty of pepper in casserole. Season lightly with salt and add nutmeg; cover and microwave 6 minutes at HIGH.

Mix well. Stir in flour until well incorporated.

Add milk, mix very well and correct seasoning. Mix in curry powder and microwave 4 minutes uncovered at HIGH.

Mix in cheese; microwave 3 minutes uncovered at MEDIUM-HIGH.

Serve over toasted French bread.

Vegetables au Gratin

(serves 4)

1 SERVING	100 CALORIES	13g CARBOHYDRATE
5g PROTEIN	3g FAT	1.7g FIBER

Setting: HIGH and MEDIUM
Cooking time: 14 minutes
Utensil: 12 cup (3 L) casserole

½	eggplant
4	green onions, chopped
1 tsp	(5 ml) vegetable oil
½	zucchini, diced small
2	garlic cloves, smashed and chopped
½ tsp	(2 ml) oregano
1 cup	(250 ml) tomato sauce
½ cup	(125 ml) grated Parmesan cheese
	salt and pepper

Slice eggplant lengthwise into ¼ in (0.65 cm) thick pieces. Dice small and place in casserole with onions and oil; season well. Cover and microwave 5 minutes at HIGH.

Add zucchini, garlic and oregano; mix and continue microwaving 3 minutes, covered.

Mix in tomato sauce and correct seasoning; cover and microwave 5 minutes.

Sprinkle in cheese, mix slightly and finish microwaving 1 minute uncovered at MEDIUM.

Place eggplant, onions and oil in casserole. Season well, cover and microwave 5 minutes at HIGH.

Mix in tomato sauce and correct seasoning; cover and microwave 5 minutes.

Add zucchini, garlic and oregano; mix and continue microwaving 3 minutes, covered.

Sprinkle in cheese, mix slightly and finish microwaving 1 minute uncovered at MEDIUM.

Shallot Baked Tomatoes

(serves 4)

1 SERVING	55 CALORIES	7g CARBOHYDRATE
0g PROTEIN	3g FAT	1.5g FIBER

Setting: HIGH

Cooking time: 5 minutes

Utensil: microwave trivet

2	large tomatoes, halved
1 tbsp	(15 ml) chopped chives
1 tbsp	(15 ml) butter
2	shallots, chopped
¼ tsp	(1 ml) Worcestershire sauce
2 tbsp	(30 ml) breadcrumbs
	salt and pepper

Set tomato halves, cut-side-up, on trivet.

Mix remaining ingredients together in small bowl until well combined.

Spread shallot butter over tomatoes and microwave 5 minutes uncovered.

Stewed Tomatoes

(serves 4)

1 SERVING	76 CALORIES	16g CARBOHYDRATE
3g PROTEIN	0g FAT	1.1g FIBER

Setting: HIGH

Cooking time: 12 minutes

Utensil: 12 cup (3 L) casserole

1 tsp	(5 ml) olive oil
2	garlic cloves, smashed and finely chopped
1	celery stalk, diced small
3 tbsp	(45 ml) finely chopped onion
¼ tsp	(1 ml) oregano
¼ tsp	(1 ml) basil
1 tsp	(5 ml) soya sauce
28 oz	(796 ml) can tomatoes, drained and chopped
4 tbsp	(60 ml) tomato paste
1 tbsp	(15 ml) honey
	salt and pepper

Place oil, garlic, celery, onion, oregano, basil, soya sauce, salt and pepper in casserole. Cover and microwave 4 minutes.

Mix well and add tomatoes, tomato paste and honey. Correct seasoning and mix again. Microwave 8 minutes uncovered, stirring twice during cooking process.

Serve stewed tomatoes with meat or use in other recipes.

Breaded Tomatoes

(serves 4)

1 SERVING	219 CALORIES	31g CARBOHYDRATE
10g PROTEIN	6g FAT	2.1g FIBER

Setting: HIGH and MEDIUM-HIGH

Cooking time: 6 minutes

Utensil: large rectangular microwave dish

3	large tomatoes, sliced ½ in (1.2 cm) thick
3	beaten eggs
1½ cups	(375 ml) seasoned breadcrumbs
½ cup	(125 ml) grated Parmesan cheese
	salt and pepper

Season tomatoes generously and dip in beaten eggs. Coat with breadcrumbs and dip slices in eggs a second time.

Place coated tomato slices in buttered rectangular dish; microwave 5 minutes uncovered at HIGH.

Sprinkle cheese over tomatoes and finish microwaving 1 minute uncovered at MEDIUM-HIGH.

Serve as vegetable garnish.

Cheesy Stuffed Tomatoes

(serves 4)

1 SERVING	221 CALORIES	16g CARBOHYDRATE
6g PROTEIN	15g FAT	2.7g FIBER

Setting: HIGH and MEDIUM-HIGH

Cooking time: 10 minutes

Utensil: 12 cup (3 L) casserole rectangular dish

4	large tomatoes
1 tbsp	(15 ml) butter
¼ cup	(50 ml) finely diced green pepper
1	carrot, pared and finely diced
½	celery stalk, finely diced
1 tbsp	(15 ml) chopped chives
1 tbsp	(15 ml) curry powder
1 cup	(250 ml) cheesy white sauce, hot
¼ cup	(50 ml) grated cheddar cheese
	salt and pepper

Place tomatoes upside-down on cutting board. Cut out small triangle-shaped caps and scoop out most of the insides with small spoon. Season shells and set aside in rectangular dish.

Place butter, vegetables, chives and curry powder in casserole. Cover with plastic wrap and microwave 4 minutes at HIGH.

Fill tomato shells with mixture and season well. Cover with plastic wrap and microwave 3 minutes at HIGH.

Pour sauce over tomatoes and top with cheese. Microwave 3 minutes uncovered at MEDIUM-HIGH.

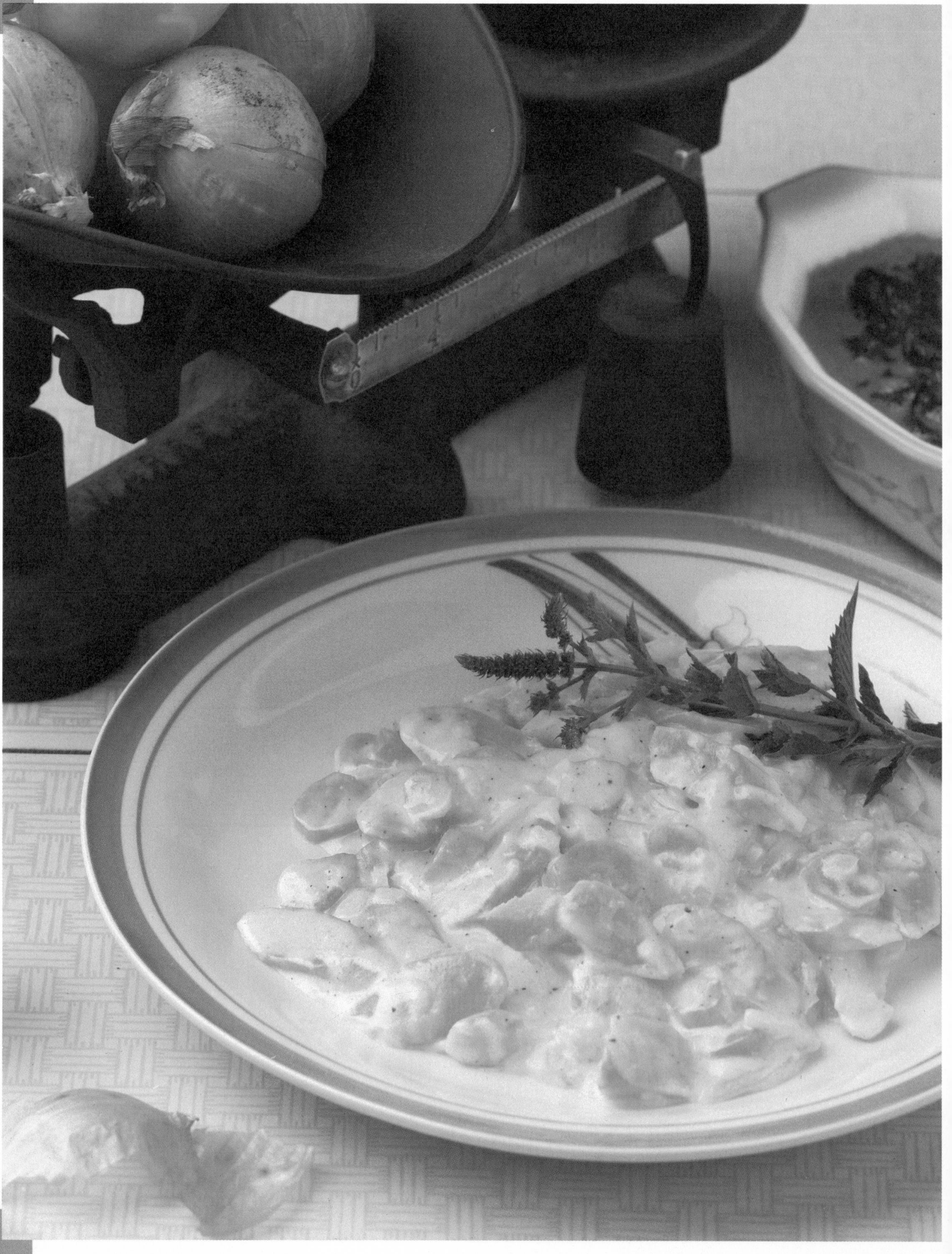

Carrots with Mint

(serves 2)

1 SERVING	212 CALORIES	21g CARBOHYDRATE
3g PROTEIN	13g FAT	3.5g FIBER

Setting: HIGH

Cooking time: 14 minutes

Utensil: 12 cup (3 L) casserole

4-5	carrots, pared and sliced on angle
½	onion, finely chopped
2 tbsp	(30 ml) butter
3-4	fresh mint leaves
½ cup	(125 ml) water
1½ tbsp	(25 ml) flour
½ cup	(125 ml) milk
	salt and pepper

Place carrots, onion and butter in casserole. Add mint, season well and pour in water.

Cover with plastic wrap and microwave 5 minutes.

Stir carrots and sprinkle in flour. Mix well and let stand 1 minute.

Add milk, stir and cover with plastic wrap; microwave 4 minutes.

Stir, correct seasoning and finish microwaving 5 minutes with cover. Serve.

Place carrots, onion and butter in casserole.

Stir carrots and sprinkle in flour. Mix well and let stand 1 minute.

Add mint, season well and pour in water.

Add milk, stir and cover with plastic wrap; microwave 4 minutes.

Perrier Carrots

(serves 2-4)

1 SERVING	114 CALORIES	15g CARBOHYDRATE
0g PROTEIN	6g FAT	2.2g FIBER

Setting: HIGH

Cooking time: 15 minutes

Utensil: 12 cup (3 L) casserole

4	large carrots, pared and thinly sliced
1 cup	(250 ml) Perrier mineral water
2	mint leaves
1	small bay leaf
2 tbsp	(30 ml) butter
2 tbsp	(30 ml) sugar
1 tbsp	(15 ml) chopped parsley
	juice ¼ lemon
	salt and pepper

Place all ingredients in casserole. Cover with plastic wrap and microwave 5 minutes.

Mix carrots, replace cover and microwave another 5 minutes.

Stir once more and finish microwaving 5 minutes covered.

Stuffed Artichoke Bottoms

(serves 4)

1 SERVING	333 CALORIES	19g CARBOHYDRATE
22g PROTEIN	19g FAT	1.3g FIBER

Setting: HIGH

Cooking time: 13 minutes

Utensil: 12 cup (3 L) casserole rectangular dish

3 tbsp	(45 ml) butter
3 tbsp	(45 ml) chopped onion
½ lb	(250 ml) mushrooms, sliced
3 tbsp	(45 ml) flour
2 cups	(500 ml) hot milk
¼ tsp	(1 ml) nutmeg
8	artichoke bottoms
1½ cups	(375 ml) crabmeat
½ cup	(125 ml) grated Gruyère cheese
	salt and pepper

Place butter, onion and mushrooms in casserole; season well. Microwave 3 minutes uncovered.

Stir and mix in flour until well incorporated.

Whisk in milk, season and add nutmeg. Microwave 8 minutes uncovered, stirring every 2 minutes.

Meanwhile, arrange artichoke bottoms in rectangular dish.

Mix ½ cup (125 ml) of mushroom sauce with crabmeat and fill artichoke bottoms with mixture.

Cover with remaining sauce and top with cheese. Microwave 2 minutes uncovered. Serve.

Stuffed Cucumber Shells

(serves 2-4)

1 SERVING	95 CALORIES	11g CARBOHYDRATE
6g PROTEIN	3g FAT	0.8g FIBER

Setting: HIGH

Cooking time: 13 minutes

Utensil: square microwave dish 12 cup (3 L) casserole

1	English cucumber
1 tbsp	(15 ml) butter
1	celery stalk, finely chopped
3 tbsp	(45 ml) chopped onion
1	garlic clove, smashed and chopped
½ cup	(125 ml) lean ground beef
½ cup	(125 ml) cooked rice
1 tbsp	(15 ml) tomato paste
1 tsp	(5 ml) Worcestershire sauce
1 tsp	(5 ml) soya sauce
⅔ cup	(150 ml) tomato sauce
	salt and pepper

Cut off ends of cucumber and slice into pieces about 1¼ in (3 cm) long. Using apple corer, remove all seeds from middle and place shells upright in square dish; set aside.

Place remaining ingredients, except tomato sauce, in casserole. Mix well, cover and microwave 4 minutes.

Mix well with whisk and spoon meat mixture into cucumber shells.

Top with tomato sauce and season well. Cover with plastic wrap and microwave 9 minutes.

Serve as an appetizer, with lunch or as a snack.

Leeks with Vinaigrette

(serves 4)

1 SERVING	169 CALORIES	6g CARBOHYDRATE
3g PROTEIN	15g FAT	0.7g FIBER

Setting: HIGH	
Cooking time: 15 minutes	
Utensil: 12 cup (3 L) casserole	
6	leeks, white part only
1 cup	(250 ml) boiling chicken stock
1 tbsp	(15 ml) lemon juice
2	hard-boiled eggs, chopped
1 tbsp	(15 ml) chopped parsley
1 tbsp	(15 ml) Dijon mustard
3 tbsp	(45 ml) wine vinegar
½ cup	(125 ml) olive oil
	salt and pepper

Place leeks, chicken stock and lemon juice in casserole; season well. Cover with plastic wrap and microwave 8 minutes. Turn leeks over; microwave 7 minutes covered.

Meanwhile, place eggs, parsley, mustard and vinegar in small bowl; season well. Mix together with whisk.

Slowly incorporate oil in thin stream while whisking constantly until well blended. Correct seasoning.

Drain leeks and arrange on serving platter. Top with vinaigrette and serve as hot vegetable with main course.

Choose the
freshest spinach
available and be sure
it is well washed.

Place spinach
in casserole with
butter and water;
season well. Cover
and microwave
4 minutes.

 After liquid
has been drained
from casserole, add
flour and milk to
spinach; mix well.
Season with nutmeg,
salt and pepper;
cover and microwave
8 minutes.

 Sprinkle in
grated cheese to
taste, stir and serve.

Spinach au Gratin

(serves 4)

1 SERVING	196 CALORIES	11g CARBOHYDRATE
11g PROTEIN	12g FAT	5.7g FIBER

Setting: HIGH	
Cooking time: 12 minutes	
Utensil: 12 cup (3 L) casserole	
2	10 oz (284 g) packages spinach, well washed
2 tbsp	(30 ml) butter
¼ cup	(50 ml) water
2 tbsp	(30 ml) flour
1 cup	(250 ml) hot milk
¼ tsp	(1 ml) nutmeg
	salt and pepper
	grated cheese to taste

Place spinach in casserole. Add butter, pour in water and season well. Cover and microwave 4 minutes.

Drain liquid from casserole. Squeeze out any excess moisture from spinach, then replace in casserole.

Mix in flour until well incorporated. Add milk, nutmeg, salt and pepper; mix, cover and microwave 4 minutes.

Stir well and continue microwaving 4 minutes, covered.

Sprinkle in cheese to taste, stir and serve as part of main meal.

How to Cook Spinach

Setting: HIGH	
Cooking time: 6 minutes	
Utensil: 12 cup (3 L) casserole	
10 oz	(284 g) package spinach
	salt

Rinse spinach under running warm water, then wash well in plenty of cold water.

Without drying spinach, place in casserole and salt lightly. Cover and microwave 6 minutes.

Remove from microwave and squeeze out excess liquid from spinach.

Serve 'au naturel' or with a cheese sauce.

Stuffed Mushrooms

(serves 4)

1 SERVING	114 CALORIES	7g CARBOHYDRATE
8g PROTEIN	6g FAT	0.7g FIBER

Setting: HIGH and MEDIUM-HIGH

Cooking time: 12 minutes

Utensil: 12 cup (3 L) casserole microwave trivet

12	large mushrooms
1 tsp	(5 ml) oil
4	anchovy filets, chopped
1	onion, finely chopped
1	garlic clove, smashed and chopped
2 tbsp	(30 ml) chopped chives
1/3 cup	(75 ml) cooked rice
1/4 cup	(50 ml) grated Gruyère cheese
	salt and pepper
	extra oil

Clean mushrooms with damp towel. Remove stems and chop; place in casserole. Set mushroom caps aside.

Add 1 tsp (5 ml) oil, anchovies, onion, garlic and chives to casserole. Cover and microwave 3 minutes at HIGH.

Mix well and season. Stir in rice and cheese; set stuffing aside.

Set mushroom caps, hollow side-up, on trivet. Brush with some oil and season well. Microwave 4 minutes uncovered at HIGH.

Drain each mushroom cap of any moisture. Fill with stuffing and microwave 5 minutes uncovered at MEDIUM-HIGH.

Serve with other appetizers if desired.

Eggplant Casserole

(serves 4)

1 SERVING	129 CALORIES	20g CARBOHYDRATE
5g PROTEIN	3g FAT	2.4g FIBER

Setting: HIGH

Cooking time: 14 minutes

Utensil: 5 cup (1.2 L) rectangular dish

1	eggplant
1	onion, chopped
2	garlic cloves, smashed and chopped
2	tomatoes, cored and sliced
1 tsp	(5 ml) olive oil
1/4 tsp	(1 ml) oregano
1 1/2 cups	(375 ml) tomato sauce
1/2 cup	(125 ml) grated Parmesan cheese
	dash paprika
	salt and pepper

Slice eggplant in half, lengthwise. Dice first half and set aside. Take remaining half and slice into 4 pieces (see technique) and using these, cover the sides, ends and bottom of rectangular dish.

Add layer of onion, garlic and tomatoes. Sprinkle in oil, oregano, paprika, salt and pepper.

Add layer of diced eggplant and pour in tomato sauce. Cover with plastic wrap and microwave 10 minutes.

Sprinkle in cheese and microwave 4 minutes uncovered.

This is delicious for lunch or serves as a very nice dinner vegetable.

Cover the sides, **1** ends and bottom of rectangular dish with slices of eggplant.

Add layer **3** of diced eggplant.

Add layer **2** of onion, garlic and tomatoes. Sprinkle in oil, oregano, paprika, salt and pepper.

Pour in **4** tomato sauce.

Asparagus and Egg Bake

(serves 4)

1 SERVING	271 CALORIES	18g CARBOHYDRATE
12g PROTEIN	17g FAT	1.4g FIBER

Setting: HIGH
Cooking time: 12 minutes
Utensil: 12 cup (3 L) casserole

3 tbsp	(45 ml) butter
1 tsp	(5 ml) chervil
1 tsp	(5 ml) finely chopped chives
3 tbsp	(45 ml) flour
2 cups	(500 ml) hot milk
¼ tsp	(1 ml) nutmeg
2	bunches fresh asparagus, trimmed and cooked
3	hard-boiled eggs, chopped
3 tbsp	(45 ml) breadcrumbs
	salt and pepper

Place butter, chervil and chives in casserole. Cover and microwave 1 minute.

Mix in flour until well incorporated.

Pour in milk with nutmeg, whisk and season well. Microwave 8 minutes uncovered, stirring every 2 minutes.

Meanwhile, arrange asparagus in buttered rectangular dish. Cover with chopped eggs and season well.

Pour in white sauce and sprinkle in breadcrumbs. Microwave 3 minutes uncovered.

Mashed Potato and Apple

(serves 4)

1 SERVING	290 CALORIES	45g CARBOHYDRATE
3g PROTEIN	11g FAT	2.6g FIBER

Setting: HIGH
Cooking time: 15 minutes
Utensil: 12 cup (3 L) casserole

3 tbsp	(45 ml) butter
4	large potatoes, peeled and sliced paper-thin
2	green apples, cored, peeled and thinly sliced
2 tbsp	(30 ml) heavy cream
	salt and pepper
	dash nutmeg
	dash paprika

Using 1 tbsp (15 ml) of butter, grease casserole. Spread sliced potatoes in bottom and pour in enough hot water to cover. Season well and microwave 8 minutes covered.

Add apples and continue microwaving 7 minutes, covered.

Drain potatoes and apples well, then force through potato ricer or food mill into bowl.

Stir in remaining butter, add cream and seasonings. Serve.

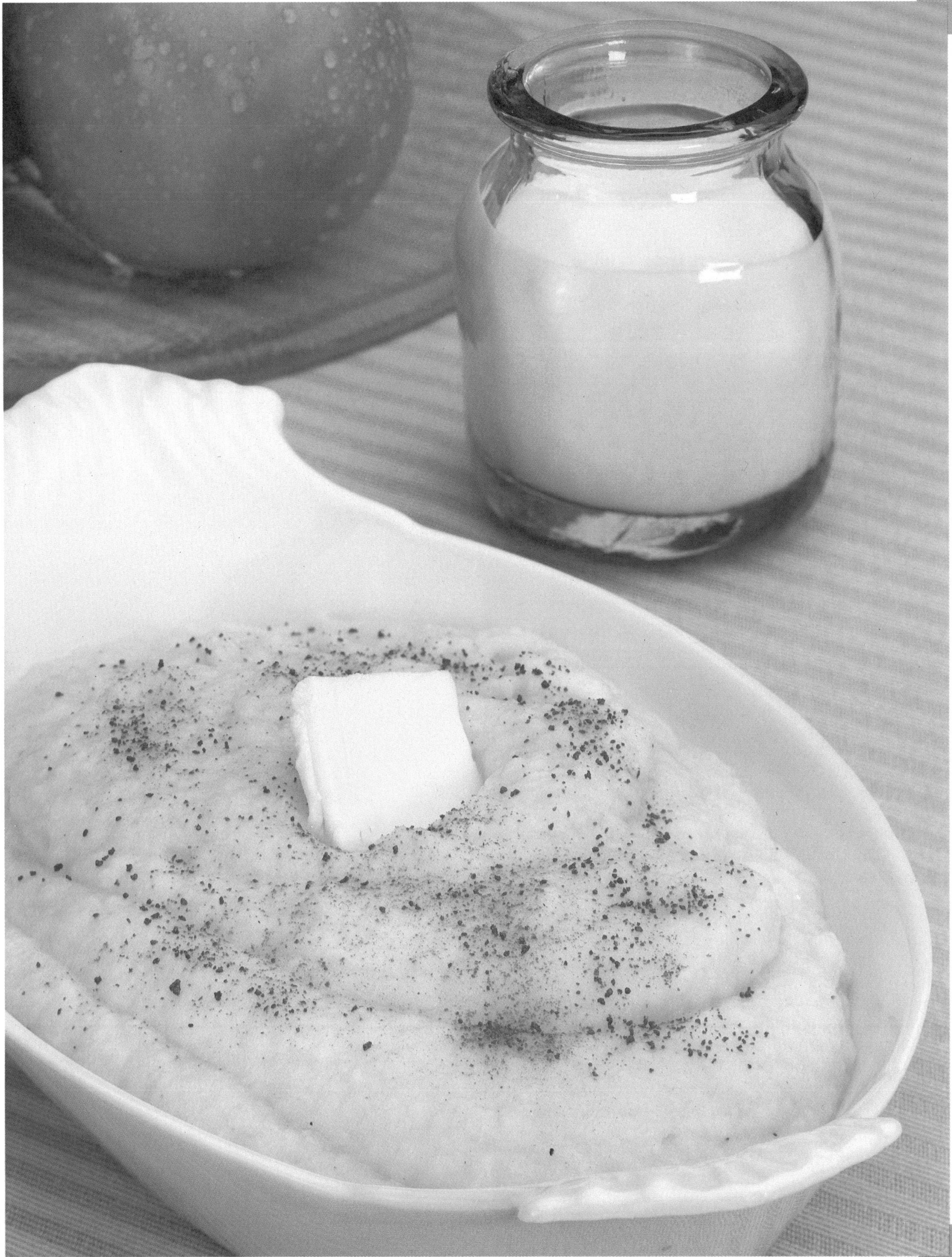

Baked Taters with Sole Topping

(serves 4)

1 SERVING	414 CALORIES	45g CARBOHYDRATE
18g PROTEIN	18g FAT	3.7g FIBER

Setting: MEDIUM-HIGH

Cooking time: 5 minutes

Utensil: 5 cup (1.2 L) rectangular dish
small baking dish

4	potatoes, baked and still hot
1 tsp	(5 ml) butter
1	large sole filet, in bite-size pieces
½	cucumber, peeled, seeded and sliced
1 tsp	(5 ml) lemon juice
1½ cups	(375 ml) thick white sauce
½ cup	(125 ml) grated Parmesan cheese
	dash paprika
	salt and pepper

Slit potatoes open and set aside in baking dish.

Place butter, sole, cucumber, lemon juice, some paprika and pepper in rectangular dish. Cover with plastic wrap and microwave 3 minutes.

Pour in white sauce, more paprika and mix well.

Spoon mixture in and over slit potatoes and top with Parmesan cheese. Microwave 2 minutes uncovered.

Place butter, sole, cucumber, lemon juice, some paprika and pepper in rectangular dish. Cover with plastic wrap and microwave 3 minutes.

Pour in white sauce, more paprika and season well.

Spoon mixture in and over slit potatoes.

Top with Parmesan cheese and microwave 2 minutes uncovered.

Tomato Potatoes

(serves 4)

1 SERVING	193 CALORIES	33g CARBOHYDRATE
4g PROTEIN	5g FAT	1.9g FIBER

Setting: HIGH

Cooking time: 15 minutes

Utensil: 12 cup (3 L) casserole

1½ tbsp	(25 ml) melted butter
2	large potatoes, peeled and sliced paper thin
1	recipe Stewed Tomatoes
	salt and pepper

Spread melted butter over bottom of casserole.

Add potatoes in one layer and season well. Cover with tomatoes and plastic wrap; microwave 6 minutes.

Rotate casserole ½ turn; continue microwaving 9 minutes, covered.

Scalloped Potatoes

(serves 4)

1 SERVING	324 CALORIES	20g CARBOHYDRATE
10g PROTEIN	23g FAT	0.9g FIBER

Setting: HIGH and MEDIUM-HIGH

Cooking time: 15 minutes

Utensil: 12 cup (3 L) casserole

2	large potatoes, peeled
¼ cup	(50 ml) melted butter
3 tbsp	(45 ml) finely chopped onion
¼ tsp	(1 ml) savory
½ cup	(125 ml) hot light cream
1 cup	(250 ml) grated cheddar cheese
	salt and pepper

Slice potatoes paper thin by using food processor or other cutting device. Place slices in plenty of cold water.

Pour butter in casserole and spread to coat bottom and part of sides.

Drain potatoes very well and layer in casserole; season generously. Sprinkle in onion and savory. Cover with plastic wrap (it should touch potatoes) and microwave 7 minutes at HIGH.

Pour in cream, then top with cheese. Microwave 8 minutes uncovered at MEDIUM-HIGH, rotating casserole twice during cooking process.

Cover casserole and let stand 3 minutes before serving.

Minty Potato Salad

(serves 4)

1 SERVING	184 CALORIES	26g CARBOHYDRATE
2g PROTEIN	8g FAT	1.2g FIBER

Setting: HIGH

Cooking time: 15 minutes

Utensil: 12 cup (3 L) casserole

5	medium potatoes, peeled and diced small
2 cups	(500 ml) boiling water
1 tbsp	(15 ml) chopped parsley
1	shallot, finely chopped
2	small mint leaves, finely chopped
¼ tsp	(1 ml) chopped fresh savory
2½ tbsp	(40 ml) wine vinegar
1 tbsp	(15 ml) Dijon mustard
2½ tbsp	(40 ml) olive oil
	salt and pepper

Place potatoes and water in casserole. Add salt and microwave 15 minutes uncovered.

Remove casserole from microwave and let stand 5 minutes.

Drain potatoes well and transfer to mixing bowl. Add parsley, shallot, mint and savory; mix.

Sprinkle in vinegar and toss. Add mustard and mix very well.

Add olive oil, mix again and season well with salt and pepper.

Marinate salad 1 hour at room temperature.

If desired garnish platter with assorted vegetable sticks, olives, etc.

Hot Vegetable Salad

(serves 4)

1 SERVING	331 CALORIES	19g CARBOHYDRATE
2g PROTEIN	28g FAT	3.0g FIBER

Setting: HIGH
Cooking time: 15 minutes
Utensil: 12 cup (3 L) casserole

3 cups	(750 ml) boiling water
2	small potatoes, peeled and diced small
2 tbsp	(30 ml) olive oil
1	medium onion, diced
½	zucchini, diced small
½	red pepper, diced small
½	yellow pepper, diced small
2	green onions, in ½ in (1.2 cm) lengths
2	slices eggplant, diced small
2	tomatoes, diced small
½	cucumber, seeded and diced small
	salt and pepper
	few drops lemon juice
	mustard vinaigrette or shallot dressing to taste

Pour boiling water into casserole, drop in potatoes and season. Cover and microwave 5 minutes.

Drain potatoes well and clean casserole. Add oil, replace potatoes and add remaining vegetables, except tomatoes and cucumber. Season well, cover and microwave 7 minutes.

Stir well. Add tomatoes and cucumber; mix, cover and microwave 3 minutes.

Remove casserole from microwave and let vegetables stand 5 minutes before adding vinaigrette.

Toss and serve.

Before microwaving, prepare the vegetables.

Microwave all vegetables, except tomatoes and cucumber, for 7 minutes covered.

Add remaining vegetables; mix, cover and microwave 3 minutes.

You can prepare your choice of vinaigrette while vegetables are standing 5 minutes.

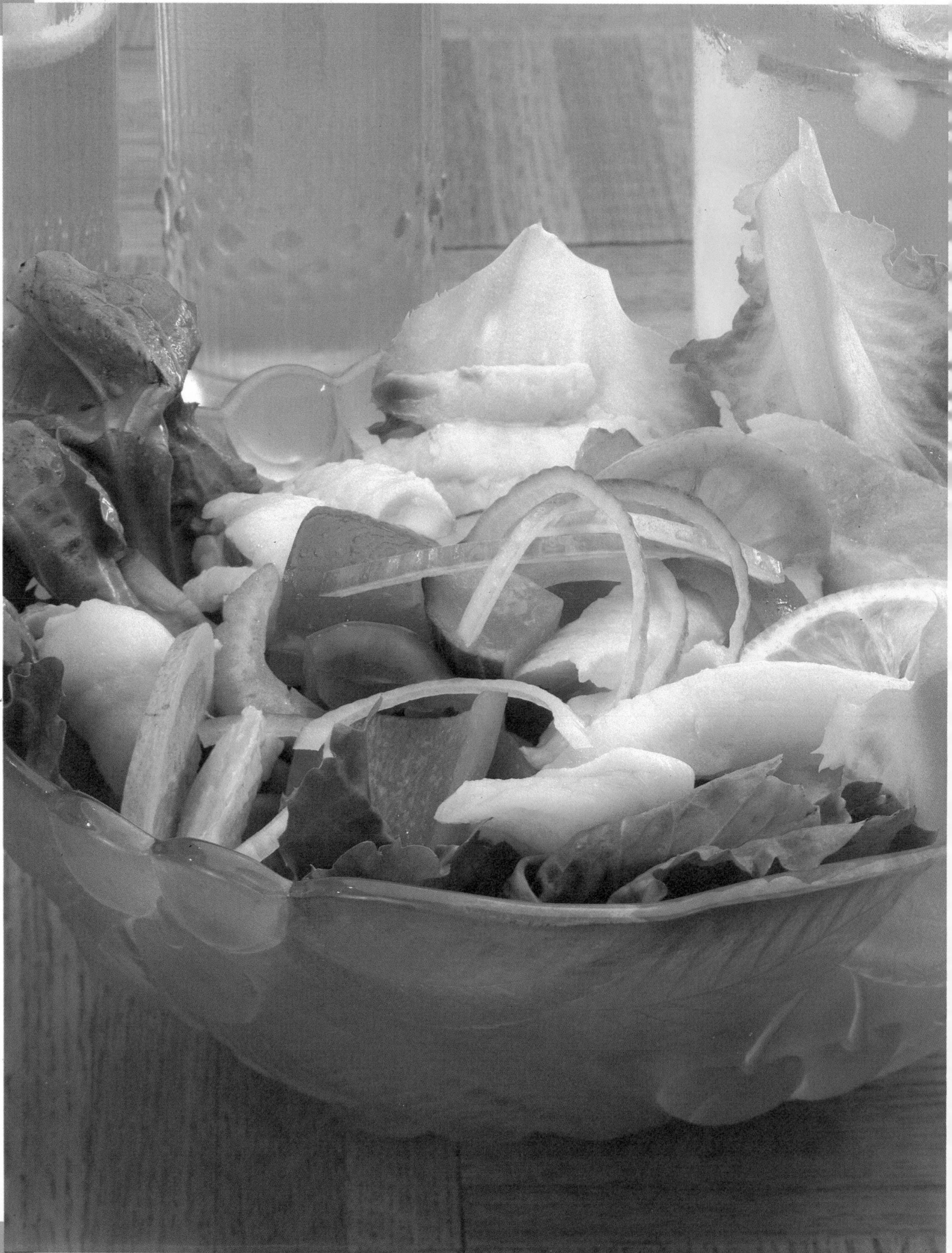

Sunnyside Sole Salad

(serves 4)

1 SERVING	167 CALORIES	5g CARBOHYDRATE
12g PROTEIN	11g FAT	0.6g FIBER

Setting: HIGH and MEDIUM-HIGH

Cooking time: 10 minutes

Utensil: 12 cup (3 L) casserole

½	green pepper, diced large
½	red pepper, diced large
1	celery stalk, sliced
1	garlic clove, smashed and chopped
⅓	English cucumber, diced large
½	red onion, diced large
½ lb	(250 g) green beans, cut in 3
3 tbsp	(45 ml) olive oil
2	large sole filets, in pieces of 1½ in (4 cm)
1 tbsp	(15 ml) chopped parsley
4 tbsp	(60 ml) red wine vinegar
	juice ½ lemon
	salt and pepper

Place peppers, celery, garlic, cucumber, onion, green beans and 1 tbsp (15 ml) oil in casserole. Cover with plastic wrap and microwave 6 minutes at HIGH.

Mix in sole; cover and microwave 4 minutes at MEDIUM-HIGH.

Remove casserole from microwave and sprinkle in parsley and remaining oil.

Pour in vinegar, add lemon juice and season to taste. Toss well and serve warm.

Place peppers, celery, garlic, cucumber, onion, green beans and 1 tbsp (15 ml) oil in casserole. Cover with plastic wrap and microwave 6 minutes at HIGH.

Mix in sole; cover and microwave 4 minutes at MEDIUM-HIGH.

Sprinkle in parsley and remaining oil.

Pour in vinegar, add lemon juice and season to taste.

Hot Lentil Salad

(serves 4)

1 SERVING	301 CALORIES	29g CARBOHYDRATE
10g PROTEIN	16g FAT	6.1g FIBER

Setting: HIGH

Cooking time: 12 minutes

Utensil: 12 cup (3 L) casserole

6-7	cauliflower flowerets
½	zucchini, sliced
½	yellow pepper, halved and sliced
3 cups	(750 ml) hot water
19 oz	(540 ml) can lentils
1	tomato, halved and sliced
14 oz	(398 ml) can artichoke hearts, drained
¼ cup	(50 ml) pickled whole or sliced beets
	salt and pepper
	vinaigrette of your choice

Place cauliflower, zucchini, yellow pepper and hot water in casserole. Season, cover with plastic wrap and microwave 9 minutes, stirring 1-2 times.

Drain vegetables and set aside in bowl.

Pour contents of lentil can into casserole. Microwave 3 minutes with cover.

Drain lentils and add to vegetables in bowl; mix well.

Season and stir in vinaigrette to taste.

Arrange sliced tomato, artichoke hearts and beets on serving platter. Serve with lentil salad.

Penne with Meat Sauce

(serves 4)

1 SERVING	481 CALORIES	45g CARBOHYDRATE
41g PROTEIN	15g FAT	1.6g FIBER

Setting: HIGH and MEDIUM-HIGH

Cooking time: 10 minutes

Utensil: 12 cup (3 L) casserole

1 tbsp	(15 ml) finely grated lemon rind
2 tbsp	(30 ml) butter
1	small onion, finely chopped
¼ tsp	(1 ml) nutmeg
1 lb	(500 g) lean ground beef
1 tsp	(5 ml) Worcestershire sauce
1 cup	(250 ml) vegetable cocktail juice
2	tomatoes, cored and chopped
3 tbsp	(45 ml) tomato paste
4 cups	(1 L) cooked hot penne
½ cup	(125 ml) grated Parmesan cheese
	salt and pepper

Place lemon rind, butter, onion, nutmeg, beef, Worcestershire sauce, salt and pepper in casserole. Microwave 4 minutes uncovered at HIGH.

Mix in vegetable cocktail, tomatoes and tomato paste; season well.

Incorporate penne and add ¾ of cheese, just sprinkling on top. Microwave 6 minutes at MEDIUM-HIGH uncovered.

Serve with remaining cheese.

Linguine Alfredo

(serves 2)

1 SERVING	715 CALORIES	96g CARBOHYDRATE
21g PROTEIN	27g FAT	1.6g FIBER

Setting: HIGH and MEDIUM

Cooking time: 7 minutes

Utensil: large glass bowl

2 tbsp	(30 ml) butter
2 tbsp	(30 ml) finely chopped onion
8	large mushrooms, sliced
½ lb	(250 g) linguine, cooked
3 tbsp	(45 ml) heavy cream
4 tbsp	(60 ml) grated Parmesan cheese
	salt and pepper
	dash paprika
	few drops lemon juice

Place butter, onion, mushrooms, seasonings and lemon juice in glass bowl. Cover with plastic wrap and microwave 4 minutes at HIGH.

Rinse linguine under hot water. Drain and add to bowl.

Mix and stir in cream, then cheese. Microwave 3 minutes uncovered at MEDIUM.

Serve immediately.

How to Cook Linguine

(serves 2)

1 SERVING	480 CALORIES	89g CARBOHYDRATE
16g PROTEIN	6g FAT	0.5g FIBER

Setting: HIGH

Cooking time: 13 minutes

Utensil: 12 cup (3 L) casserole

4 cups	(1 L) boiling water
¼ tsp	(1 ml) salt
1 tsp	(5 ml) vinegar
½ lb	(250 g) linguine

Pour boiling water into casserole; add salt and vinegar.

Place linguine in water and stir. Microwave 5 minutes uncovered.

Stir pasta again; continue microwaving 5 minutes.

Stir pasta once more, return to microwave and cook 3 minutes.

Immediately drain linguine and rinse under cold water.

Use in a variety of recipes.

Tortellini and Vegetables

(serves 4)

1 SERVING	624 CALORIES	55g CARBOHYDRATE
25g PROTEIN	34g FAT	2.1g FIBER

Setting: HIGH

Cooking time: 11 minutes

Utensil: 12 cup (3 L) casserole

1 tbsp	(15 ml) butter
½ lb	(250 g) mushrooms, diced
1	red pepper, diced small
2	shallots, chopped
½ cup	(125 ml) cooked green peas
2 cups	(500 ml) cheese sauce, heated
½ cup	(125 ml) tomato sauce, heated
1 lb	(500 g) package tortellini, cooked (meat or cheese filling)
	salt and pepper

Place butter, mushrooms, red pepper and shallots in casserole; season well. Cover and microwave 4 minutes.

Add peas and both heated sauces; season well. Microwave 4 minutes uncovered.

Stir in tortellini and microwave 3 minutes uncovered.

If desired serve with grated cheese at the table.

Pasta Casserole

(serves 4)

1 SERVING	848 CALORIES	42g CARBOHYDRATE
63g PROTEIN	48g FAT	1.8g FIBER

Setting: HIGH

Cooking time: 15 minutes

Utensil: 12 cup (3 L) casserole

2 tbsp	(30 ml) butter
1	medium onion, chopped
1	garlic clove, smashed and chopped
1	green pepper, diced
1 lb	(500 g) lean ground beef
1	small zucchini, diced
2½ cups	(625 ml) cooked pasta (macaroni, shells, etc.)
1 cup	(250 ml) hot tomato sauce
1 cup	(250 ml) hot white sauce
1 cup	(250 ml) ricotta cheese
¼ tsp	(1 ml) nutmeg
	salt and pepper

Place butter, onion, garlic, green pepper and beef in casserole; season well. Cover and microwave 3 minutes.

Stir in zucchini and pasta. Add remaining ingredients, season and mix well. Microwave 6 minutes uncovered.

Mix well again and finish microwaving 6 minutes uncovered.

Macaroni and Cheese

(serves 2)

1 SERVING	596 CALORIES	49g CARBOHYDRATE
22g PROTEIN	35g FAT	0.3g FIBER

Setting: MEDIUM-HIGH

Cooking time: 10 minutes

Utensil: 12 cup (3 L) casserole

1 tbsp	(15 ml) butter
2½ cups	(625 ml) leftover cooked macaroni
½ cup	(125 ml) grated Gruyère cheese
1 cup	(250 ml) hot light cream
¼ cup	(50 ml) grated cheddar cheese
	salt and pepper

Place butter in casserole and add macaroni; season well. Stir in Gruyère cheese and cream; microwave 7 minutes uncovered.

Add cheddar cheese, mix well and correct seasoning. Finish microwaving 3 minutes.

Macaroni Caruso

(serves 4)

1 SERVING	405 CALORIES	50g CARBOHYDRATE
16g PROTEIN	16g FAT	1.3g FIBER

Setting: HIGH

Cooking time: 8 minutes

Utensil: 12 cup (3 L) casserole

2 tbsp	(30 ml) butter
1	onion, chopped
2	garlic cloves, smashed and chopped
½ lb	(250 g) mushrooms, thinly sliced
1 tbsp	(15 ml) chopped parsley
4 cups	(1 L) cooked hot macaroni
2 cups	(500 ml) hot tomato sauce
1 cup	(250 ml) grated cheddar cheese
1 tsp	(5 ml) Worcestershire sauce
	salt and pepper

Place butter, onion, garlic, mushrooms and parsley in casserole; cover and microwave 4 minutes.

Mix in remaining ingredients and finish microwaving 4 minutes uncovered.

Serve for lunch or as a quick dinner.

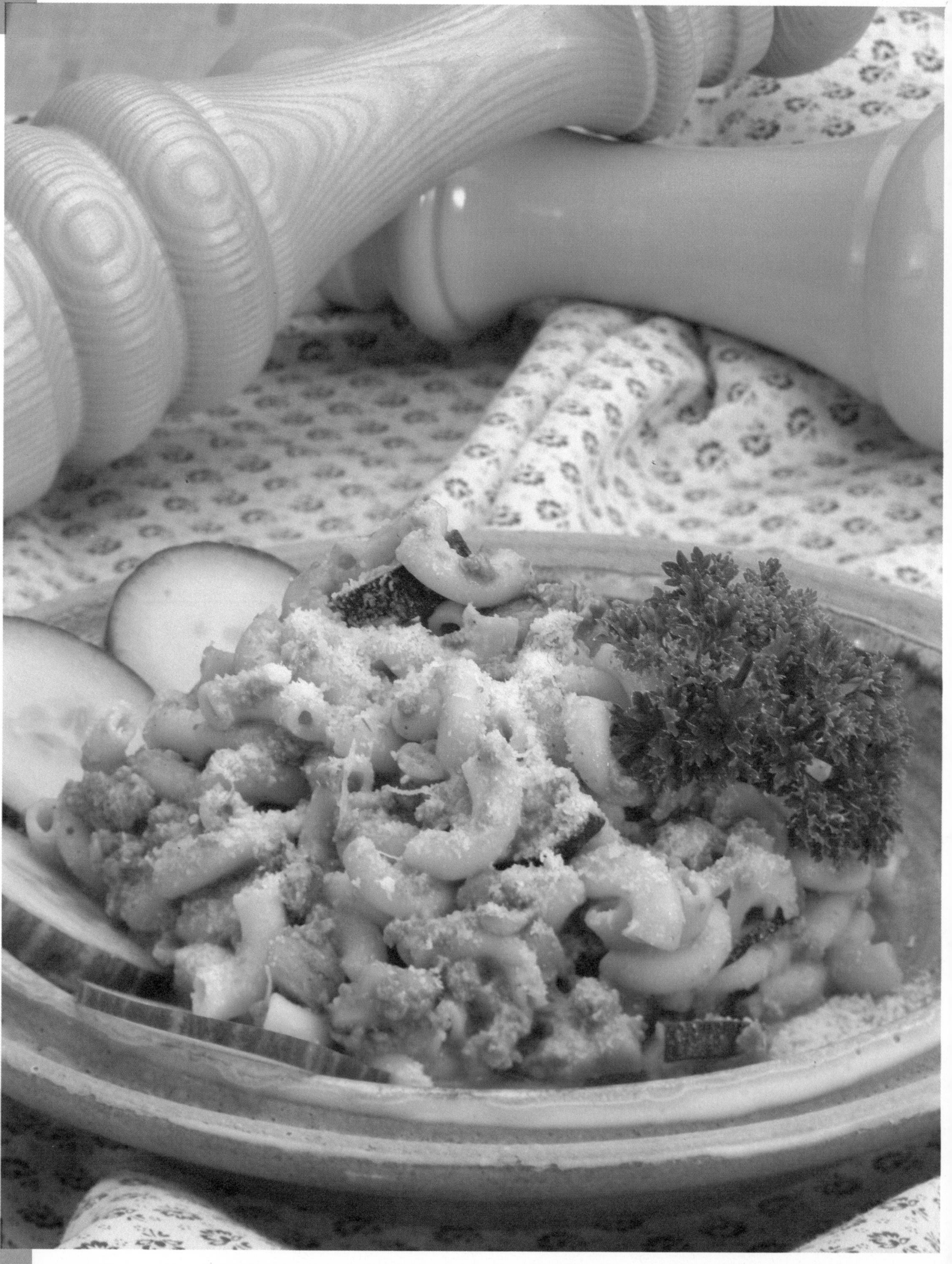

Vegetable Macaroni

(serves 4)

1 SERVING	452 CALORIES	43g CARBOHYDRATE
32g PROTEIN	17g FAT	1.3g FIBER

Setting: HIGH
Cooking time: 11 minutes
Utensil: 12 cup (3 L) casserole

2 tbsp	(30 ml) butter
1	small red onion, chopped
½	zucchini, finely diced
⅓ lb	(150 g) mushrooms, chopped
½ tsp	(2 ml) allspice
¾ lb	(375 g) lean ground beef
1 cup	(250 ml) tomato clam juice
2 tbsp	(30 ml) tomato paste
4 cups	(1 L) cooked hot elbow macaroni
¼ cup	(50 ml) heavy cream
	salt and pepper

Place butter, onion, zucchini, mushrooms and allspice in casserole. Season, cover with plastic wrap and microwave 4 minutes.

Mix well and stir in beef. Add tomato clam juice and correct seasoning.

Mix in tomato paste and microwave 5 minutes uncovered.

Incorporate pasta, then mix in cream and season. Microwave 2 minutes uncovered.

If desired serve with your favorite grated cheese.

Spaghetti with Pesto Sauce

(serves 2)

1 SERVING	1019 CALORIES	90g CARBOHYDRATE
20g PROTEIN	65g FAT	0.5g FIBER

Setting: HIGH	
Cooking time: 13 minutes	
Utensil: 12 cup (3 L) casserole	
4	sprigs fresh basil
2	large sprigs fresh parsley
½ cup	(125 ml) grated Parmesan cheese
3	garlic cloves, smashed and chopped
½ cup	(125 ml) olive oil
4 cups	(1 L) boiling water
¼ tsp	(1 ml) salt
1 tsp	(5 ml) wine vinegar
½ lb	(250 g) spaghetti or linguine

Place fresh herbs in food processor and blend until chopped. Add cheese and blend again. Add garlic and blend.

Incorporate oil in thin stream while blending. Pesto sauce should be smooth and quite thick. Set aside.

Pour boiling water into casserole; add salt and vinegar.

Place spaghetti in water and stir. Microwave 5 minutes uncovered.

Stir pasta again; continue microwaving 5 minutes uncovered.

Stir pasta once more and return to microwave for 3 minutes uncovered.

Meanwhile, pour pesto sauce into large bowl.

When spaghetti is cooked, immediately drain and rinse. Place pasta in pesto sauce, toss and serve.

Place fresh herbs in food processor.

Blend until chopped.

Add cheese and blend again.

Add garlic and blend.

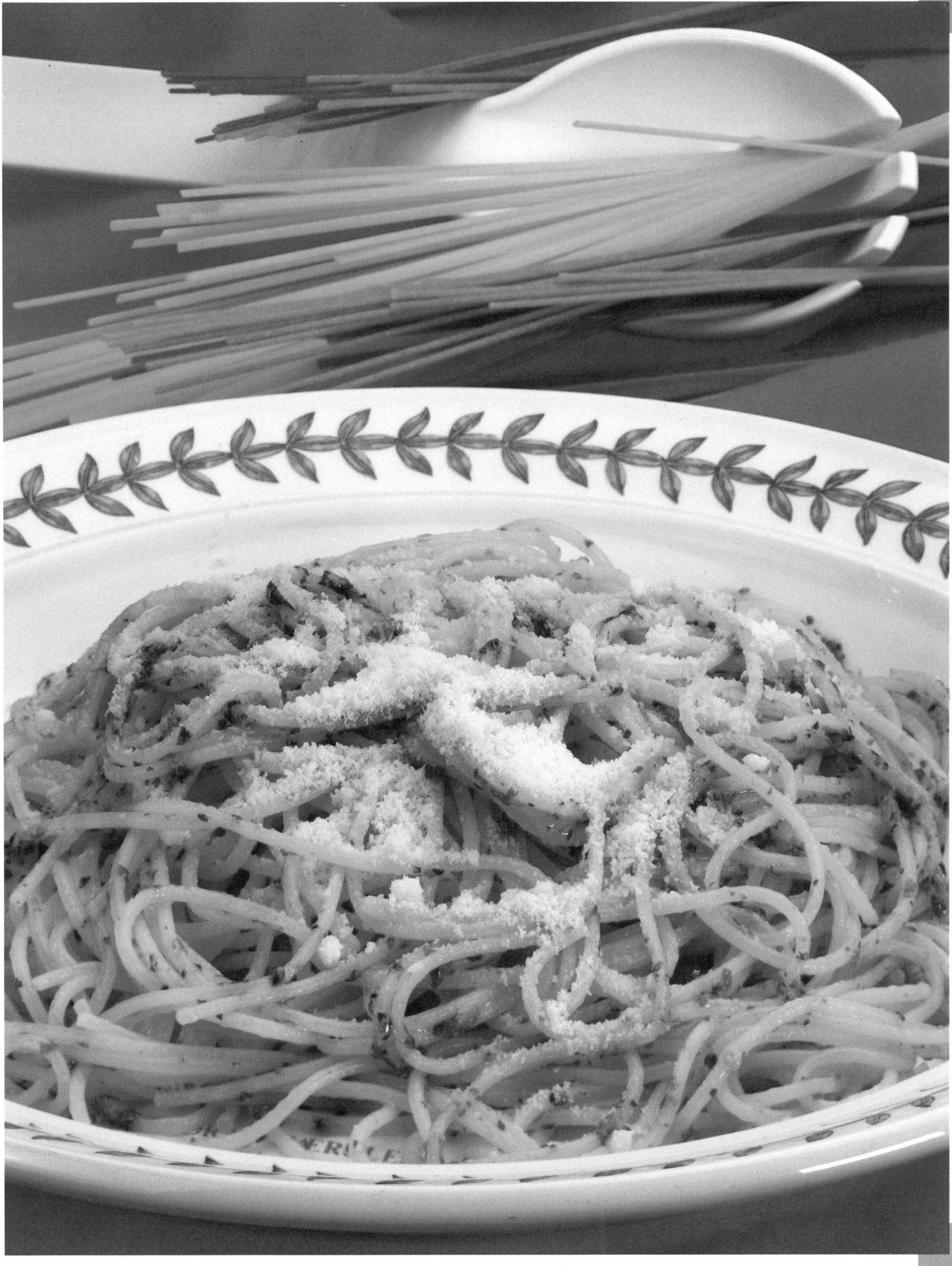

Spaghetti with Mushroom Wine Sauce

(serves 4)

1 SERVING	490 CALORIES	64g CARBOHYDRATE
31g PROTEIN	12g FAT	1.5g FIBER

Setting: HIGH
Cooking time: 12 minutes
Utensil: 12 cup (3 L) casserole

1 tbsp	(15 ml) butter
1	small onion, chopped
1	garlic clove, smashed and chopped
1 tsp	(5 ml) oregano
½ tsp	(2 ml) basil
½ lb	(250 g) lean ground beef
¼ cup	(50 ml) dry red wine
3 cups	(750 ml) tomato sauce
½ lb	(250 g) mushrooms, quartered
4	portions cooked spaghetti
½ cup	(125 ml) grated Parmesan cheese
	salt and pepper

Place butter, onion, garlic and seasonings in casserole. Cover with plastic wrap and microwave 3 minutes.

Add meat and mix well. Pour in wine and microwave 2 minutes uncovered.

Stir in tomato sauce and mushrooms; correct seasoning. Microwave 7 minutes uncovered.

Serve over spaghetti and top with cheese.

How to Cook Spiral Pasta

(serves 2)

1 SERVING	700 CALORIES	113g CARBOHYDRATE
21g PROTEIN	18g FAT	3.1g FIBER

Setting: HIGH
Cooking time: 13 minutes

Utensil: 12 cup (3 L) casserole	
4 cups	(1 L) boiling water
1 tsp	(5 ml) vegetable oil
½ lb	(250 g) spiral pasta
1	recipe vegetable sauce
	salt

Pour boiling water into casserole; add oil and salt.

Place pasta in water and stir. Microwave 6 minutes uncovered.

Stir pasta well; continue microwaving 7 minutes.

Remove casserole from microwave and let pasta stand in hot liquid 3 minutes before draining.

Rinse pasta and serve with vegetable sauce.

Pour boiling water into casserole; add oil and salt. (For spicier pasta, add pepper too.) **1**

Stir pasta well and continue microwaving 7 minutes. **3**

Place pasta in water and stir. Microwave 6 minutes uncovered. **2**

After pasta has stood 3 minutes, drain and rinse, and mix with vegetable sauce. **4**

Quick Scrambled Eggs

(serves 2)

1 SERVING	262 CALORIES	17g CARBOHYDRATE
13g PROTEIN	16g FAT	1.8g FIBER

Setting: HIGH
Cooking time: 5½ minutes
Utensil: 8 cup (2 L) divided casserole

2 tsp	(10 ml) butter
¼ cup	(50 ml) chopped red pepper
¼ cup	(50 ml) chopped English cucumber
4	eggs, well beaten
	toast
	salt and pepper

Divide butter and vegetables between the two sides of casserole. Cover with plastic wrap and microwave 3 minutes.

Add beaten eggs to each side of casserole and season well. Microwave 1 minute uncovered.

Mix very well and continue microwaving 1 minute.

Mix once more and continue microwaving ½ minute.

Stir eggs, let stand ½ minute before serving and accompany with toast.

Scrambled Eggs for Two

(serves 2)

1 SERVING	225 CALORIES	5g CARBOHYDRATE
13g PROTEIN	17g FAT	1.1g FIBER

Setting: HIGH
Cooking time: 7½ minutes
Utensil: 12 cup (3 L) casserole

½	green pepper, diced small
½	tomato, diced small
1	¼ in (0.65 cm) slice eggplant, diced small
1 tbsp	(15 ml) butter
4	eggs, well beaten
	salt and pepper
	toast

Place vegetables and butter in casserole. Season, cover with plastic wrap and microwave 5 minutes.

Mix vegetables and pour in beaten eggs; mix again. Microwave 1 minute uncovered.

Mix very well, season and continue microwaving 1 minute.

Mix once more and microwave ½ minute.

Stir eggs, let stand ½ minute before serving and accompany with toast and fruit salad if desired.

Eggs Mornay

(serves 4)

1 SERVING	419 CALORIES	19g CARBOHYDRATE
19g PROTEIN	30g FAT	0.6g FIBER

Setting: HIGH and MEDIUM-HIGH

Cooking time: 8 minutes

Utensil: oval baking dish

5	hard-boiled eggs, sliced
1 cup	(250 ml) cooked Parisienne potatoes
1½ cups	(375 ml) cheesy white sauce
¼ tsp	(1 ml) nutmeg
½ cup	(125 ml) grated cheddar cheese
	salt and pepper

Grease baking dish with butter.

Arrange eggs and potatoes in dish and pour in white sauce. Season with nutmeg, salt and pepper. Microwave 5 minutes uncovered at HIGH.

Sprinkle in cheese and microwave 3 minutes uncovered at MEDIUM-HIGH.

Serve with fresh bread.

Marvelous Muffins

1 SERVING	202 CALORIES	23g CARBOHYDRATE
3g PROTEIN	11g FAT	2.1g FIBER

Setting: HIGH
Cooking time: 2¼ minutes
Utensil: round muffin mold

1 cup	(250 ml) natural wheat bran
1 cup	(250 ml) milk
2	eggs
½ cup	(125 ml) vegetable oil
¼ cup	(50 ml) brown sugar
¼ cup	(50 ml) corn syrup
¼ cup	(50 ml) Sultana raisins
1	carrot, shredded
1⅓ cups	(325 ml) all-purpose flour
2 tsp	(10 ml) baking powder
½ tsp	(2 ml) baking soda
1 tsp	(5 ml) cinnamon
	pinch salt

Place bran in large bowl. Pour in milk and mix.

Add eggs and whisk well.

Add oil, sugar, corn syrup and raisins; mix again. Fold in carrot and set aside.

Mix flour, baking powder and soda, cinnamon and salt together in small bowl.

Fold into bran mixture and incorporate well.

Fill muffin cups ½ full and microwave 1 minute uncovered.

Rotate mold ¼ turn; continue microwaving 1 minute 15 seconds.

Remove mold from microwave and let stand 15 minutes.

Serve muffins for breakfast, brunch or dessert.

Place bran in large bowl. Pour in milk and mix.

Add eggs and whisk well.

Add oil, sugar, corn syrup and raisins; mix again. Fold in carrot and set aside.

Fold flour into bran mixture and incorporate well.

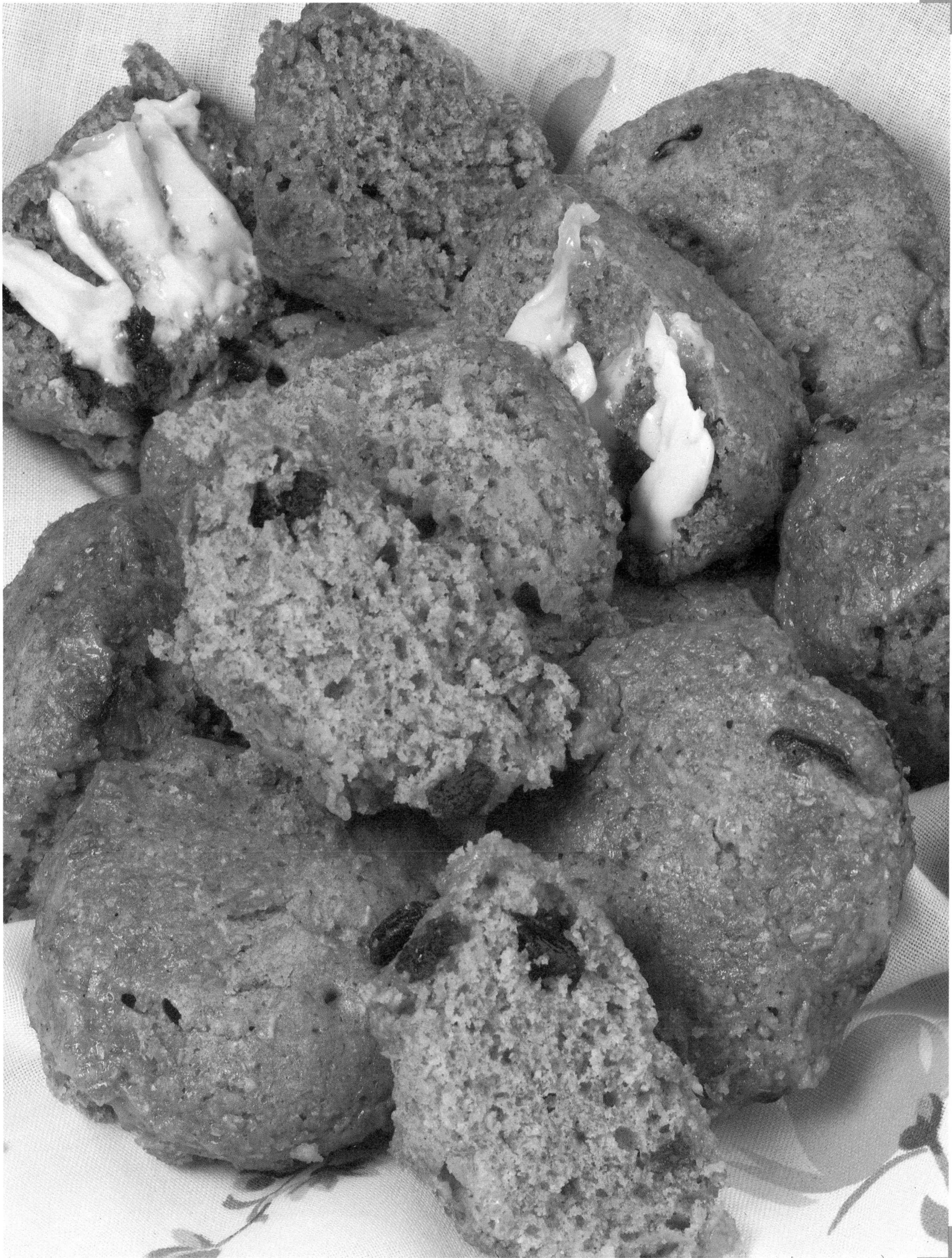

Salmon Puffs

(serves 6)

1 SERVING	148 CALORIES	9g CARBOHYDRATE
10g PROTEIN	8g FAT	1.0g FIBER

Setting: MEDIUM-HIGH

Cooking time: 6 minutes

Utensil: microwave muffin pan

7.5 oz	(213 g) can sockeye salmon, well drained
12 oz	(341 ml) can whole kernel corn, well drained
3 tbsp	(45 ml) relish
¼ cup	(50 ml) heavy cream
1 tsp	(5 ml) Worcestershire sauce
1 tsp	(5 ml) lemon juice
1	egg yolk
2	egg whites, beaten stiff salt and pepper

Place salmon, corn and relish in food processor. Blend 1 minute, taking time to scrape down sides of bowl.

Add cream and continue blending 30 seconds.

Add Worcestershire, lemon juice, salt and pepper; blend another 10 seconds.

Add egg yolk and finish blending 30 seconds.

Transfer mixture to mixing bowl and fold in beaten egg whites.

Fill cups of muffin pan about ¾ full or a little less than level depending on the size.

Microwave 6 minutes uncovered.

To unmold, run knife around edges and let stand 1 minute or so before completely removing. Serve as first course or light main course.

Vegetable Muffins

(serves 4-6)

1 SERVING	88 CALORIES	6g CARBOHYDRATE
5g PROTEIN	5g FAT	2.0g FIBER

Setting: HIGH

Cooking time: 6 minutes

Utensil: microwave muffin pan

1 cup	(250 ml) cooked spinach, well drained and chopped
1	small head cooked cauliflower, chopped
½ cup	(125 ml) white sauce
¼ tsp	(1 ml) nutmeg
2	egg yolks
2	egg whites, beaten stiff salt and pepper

Mix spinach with cauliflower, white sauce, nutmeg, salt and pepper.

Stir in egg yolks until well combined.

Fold in beaten egg whites and spoon mixture into cups of greased muffin pan.

Microwave 3 minutes. Rotate muffin pan; continue microwaving another 3 minutes.

Remove and let cool 1 minute before unmolding. Serve with chicken, fish, etc.

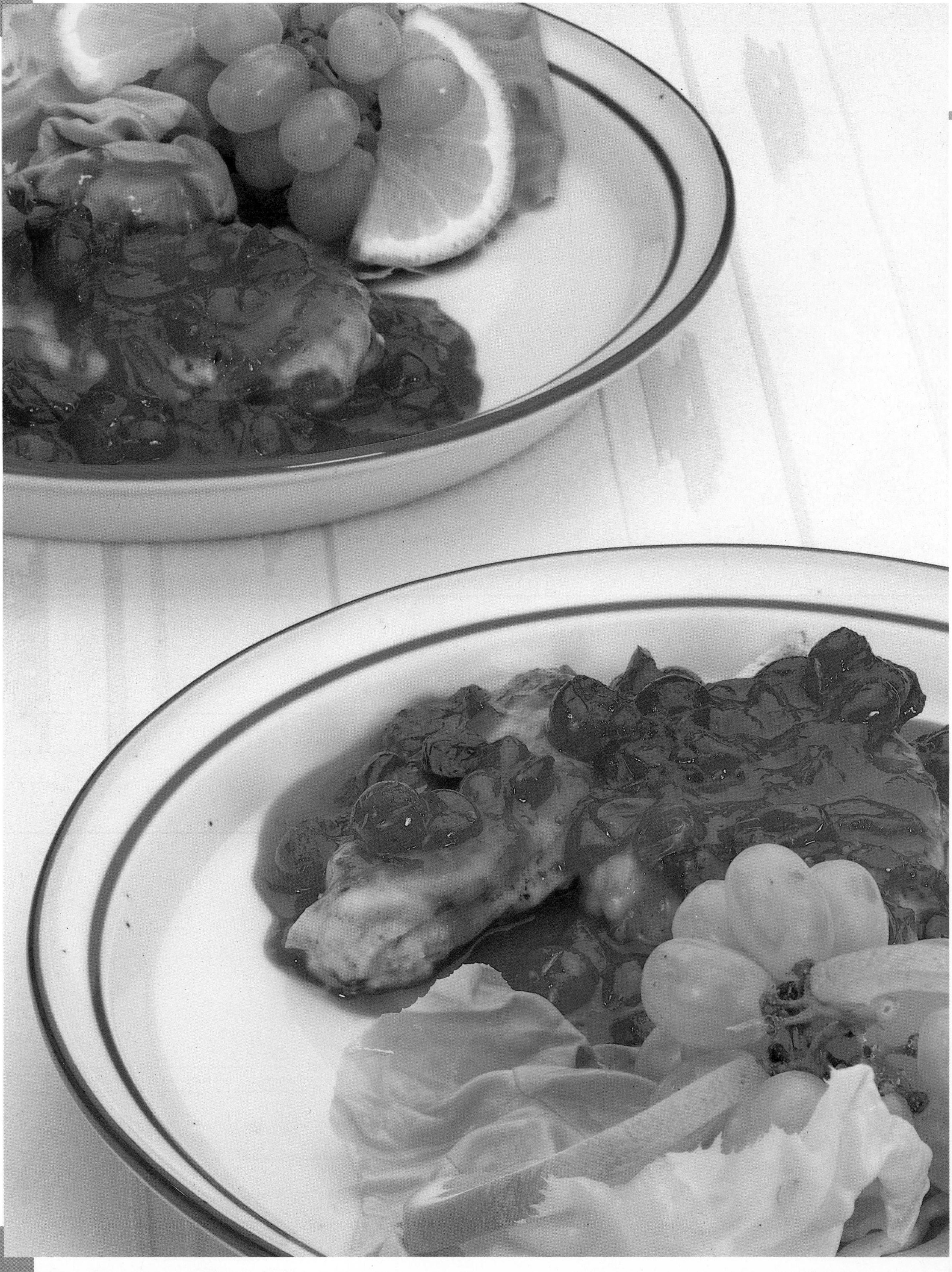

Cranberry Sauce

¼ CUP (50 ml)	52 CALORIES	13g CARBOHYDRATE
0g PROTEIN	0g FAT	0.2g FIBER

Setting: HIGH
Cooking time: 15 minutes
Utensil: 12 cup (3 L) casserole

3 cups	(750 ml) fresh or frozen cranberries, thawed
1 cup	(250 ml) sugar
1 cup	(250 ml) water
2 tbsp	(30 ml) grated lemon rind
1 tbsp	(15 ml) grated orange rind
1½ tbsp	(25 ml) cornstarch
2 tbsp	(30 ml) cold water

Place berries, sugar, 1 cup (250 ml) water and grated rinds in casserole. Microwave 13 minutes uncovered, stirring occasionally.

Mix cornstarch with 2 tbsp (30 ml) water; stir into sauce. Continue microwaving 2 minutes uncovered.

Serve over poulty.

Curried Coconut Sauce

¼ CUP (50 ml)	48 CALORIES	4g CARBOHYDRATE
1g PROTEIN	3g FAT	0.2g FIBER

Setting: HIGH
Cooking time: 15 minutes
Utensil: 12 cup (3 L) casserole

2 cups	(500 ml) light chicken stock, hot
1 cup	(250 ml) shredded coconut
2 tbsp	(30 ml) vegetable oil
2	small onions, finely chopped
1	garlic clove, smashed and chopped
3 tbsp	(45 ml) curry powder
¼ tsp	(1 ml) ground ginger
2 tbsp	(30 ml) flour
	salt and pepper

Pour chicken stock into casserole and add coconut. Microwave 3 minutes uncovered.

Strain liquid into bowl and set aside.

Clean casserole and add oil. Mix in onions and garlic; cover and microwave 2 minutes.

Add curry powder and ginger; mix very well. Microwave 2 minutes covered.

Mix in flour until well incorporated.

Add reserved chicken stock and correct seasoning. Microwave 8 minutes uncovered, stirring every 2 minutes.

Serve sauce with fish or veal.

Sweet 'n Sour Sauce

¼ CUP (50 ml)	86 CALORIES	20g CARBOHYDRATE
1g PROTEIN	0g FAT	0.1g FIBER

Setting: HIGH

Cooking time: 15 minutes

Utensil: 12 cup (3 L) casserole

1 cup	(250 ml) hot water
1 cup	(250 ml) brown sugar
¼ cup	(50 ml) white vinegar
1 cup	(250 ml) catsup
3 tbsp	(45 ml) soya sauce
2 tbsp	(30 ml) cornstarch
4 tbsp	(60 ml) cold water
	juice 1½ lemons
	freshly ground pepper

Place hot water, sugar and vinegar in casserole; mix well. Microwave 5 minutes uncovered.

Whisk in catsup. Add lemon juice, soya sauce and pepper to taste. Stir and microwave 3 minutes uncovered.

Whisk sauce well; continue microwaving 4 minutes uncovered.

Mix cornstarch with cold water; incorporate into sauce. Microwave 2 minutes uncovered.

Stir sauce once more and finish microwaving 1 minute uncovered.

Serve with chicken wings, meatballs or other meat dishes.

Meat Sauce for Pasta

(serves 4)

1 SERVING	190 CALORIES	7g CARBOHYDRATE
14g PROTEIN	12g FAT	0.3g FIBER

Setting: HIGH

Cooking time: 15 minutes

Utensil: 12 cup (3 L) casserole

1 tbsp	(15 ml) oil
1	celery stalk, diced small
3 tbsp	(45 ml) finely chopped onion
2	garlic cloves, smashed and chopped
½ lb	(250 g) lean ground beef
¼ tsp	(1 ml) oregano
¼ tsp	(1 ml) basil
4 tbsp	(60 ml) tomato paste
1 tsp	(5 ml) soya sauce
1 tbsp	(15 ml) honey
	salt and pepper

Place all ingredients in casserole and mix well. Cover and microwave 7 minutes.

Mix very well and continue microwaving 8 minutes, covered.

Serve meat sauce with a variety of pasta dishes.

Vegetable Sauce

1 SERVING	236 CALORIES	24g CARBOHYDRATE
6g PROTEIN	13g FAT	2.6g FIBER

Setting: MEDIUM and HIGH

Cooking time: 15 minutes

Utensil: 12 cup (3 L) casserole

1 tbsp	(15 ml) oil
3 tbsp	(45 ml) chopped onion
½	stalk celery, diced
2	garlic cloves, smashed and chopped
½ tsp	(2 ml) oregano
28 oz	(796 ml) can tomatoes, drained and chopped
3 tbsp	(45 ml) tomato paste
½ cup	(125 ml) pitted black olives
½ tsp	(2 ml) sugar
	dash ground hot peppers
	salt and pepper

Place oil, onion, celery, garlic and oregano in casserole. Cover and microwave 3 minutes at MEDIUM.

Add remaining ingredients and mix well. Microwave 6 minutes uncovered at HIGH.

Mix well; continue microwaving another 6 minutes uncovered at HIGH. Stir once during cooking time.

Serve with pasta.

Cheesy White Sauce

½ CUP (125 ml)	264 CALORIES	13g CARBOHYDRATE
9g PROTEIN	20g FAT	0.1g FIBER

Setting: HIGH

Cooking time: 10 minutes

Utensil: 12 cup (3 L) casserole

4 tbsp	(60 ml) butter
2 tbsp	(30 ml) chopped red onion
¼ tsp	(1 ml) nutmeg
4 tbsp	(60 ml) flour
2 cups	(500 ml) boiling milk
½ cup	(125 ml) grated cheddar cheese
	salt and pepper

Place butter, onion and nutmeg in casserole; microwave 2 minutes uncovered.

Mix in flour until well incorporated.

Add boiling milk and whisk well; correct seasoning. Microwave 6 minutes uncovered, stirring every 2 minutes.

Stir in cheese and finish microwaving 2 minutes uncovered.

Serve with a variety of recipes.

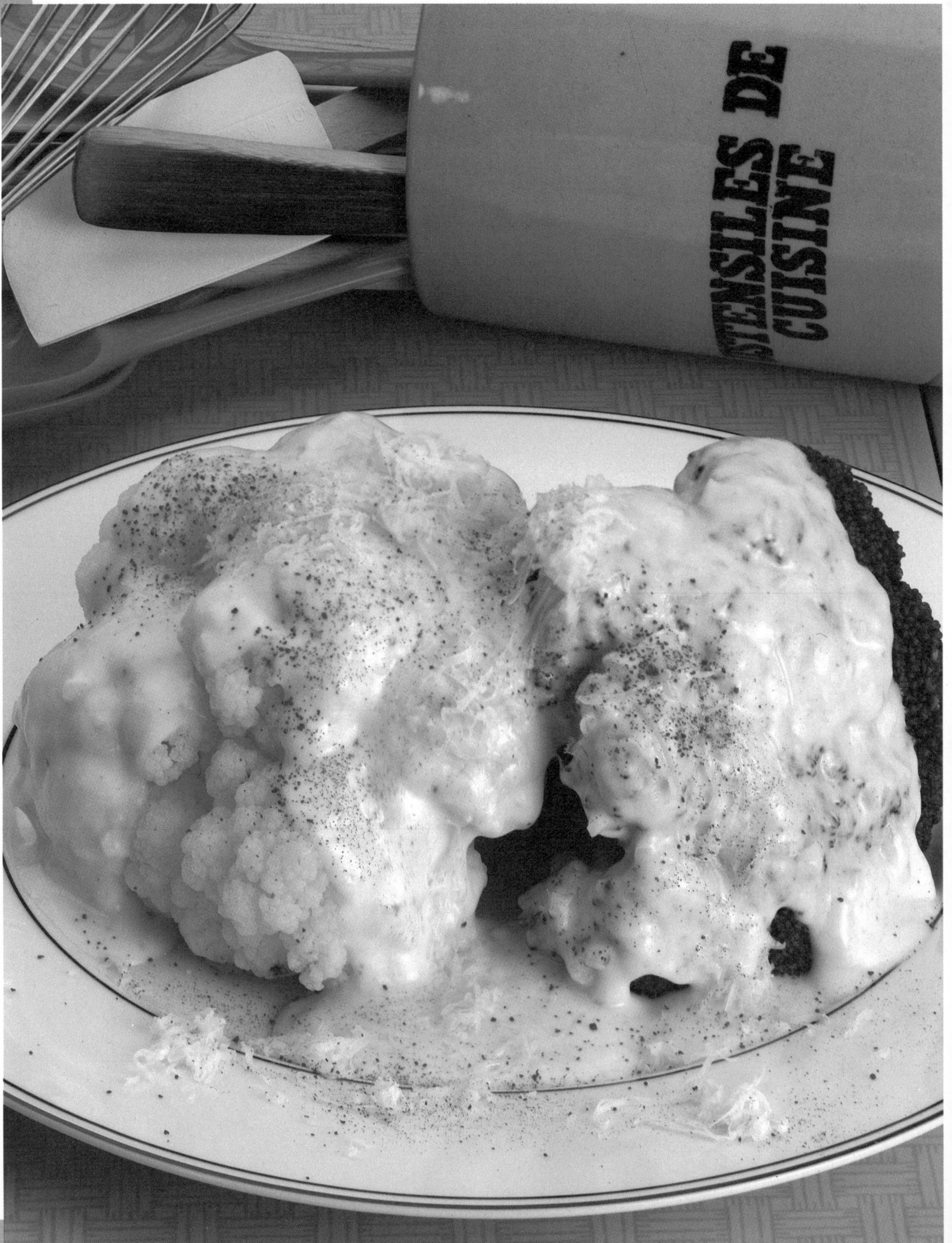
USTENSILES DE
CUISINE

Versatile White Sauce

½ CUP (125 ml)	262 CALORIES	13g CARBOHYDRATE
9g PROTEIN	20g FAT	0.1g FIBER

Setting: HIGH
Cooking time: 8 minutes
Utensil: 12 cup (3 L) casserole

4 tbsp	(60 ml) butter
2 tbsp	(30 ml) chopped onion
¼ tsp	(1 ml) paprika
4 tbsp	(60 ml) flour
2 cups	(500 ml) boiling milk
¼ tsp	(1 ml) nutmeg
½ cup	(125 ml) grated cheese (optional)
	salt and pepper

Place butter, onion and paprika in casserole; microwave 2 minutes uncovered.

Mix in flour until well incorporated.

Add boiling milk and nutmeg; whisk well and correct seasoning. Microwave 6 minutes uncovered, stirring every 2 minutes.

Serve as white sauce or if desired, stir in grated cheese for variation, without further microwaving.

This sauce is ideal for vegetables such as broccoli and cauliflower.

Place butter, onion and paprika in casserole; microwave 2 minutes uncovered.

Mix in flour until well incorporated.

Add boiling milk and nutmeg; whisk well and correct seasoning. Microwave 6 minutes uncovered, stirring every 2 minutes.

If desired, stir in grated cheese for variation without further microwaving.

Mustard Vinaigrette

1 TBSP (15 ml)	88 CALORIES	0g CARBOHYDRATE
0g PROTEIN	10g FAT	0g FIBER

1 tbsp	(15 ml) Dijon mustard
1	garlic clove, smashed and chopped
1 tsp	(5 ml) chopped tarragon
¼ tsp	(1 ml) anise
1	egg yolk
4 tbsp	(60 ml) wine vinegar
¾ cup	(175 ml) olive oil
	few drops lemon juice
	salt and pepper

In bowl, mix together mustard, garlic, tarragon, anise and egg yolk.

Add vinegar and whisk well. Stir in lemon juice and season to taste.

Incorporate oil in thin stream while whisking constantly.

Correct seasoning and serve vinaigrette with vegetables.

Shallot Dressing

1 TBSP (15 ml)	71 CALORIES	0g CARBOHYDRATE
0g PROTEIN	8g FAT	0g FIBER

2 tbsp	(30 ml) Dijon mustard
1 tbsp	(15 ml) finely chopped shallot
1 tbsp	(15 ml) chopped parsley
1 tsp	(5 ml) chopped fresh tarragon
¼ cup	(50 ml) wine vinegar
¾ cup	(175 ml) olive oil
	few drops lemon juice
	salt and pepper

In small bowl, whisk together mustard, shallot, parsley, tarragon and vinegar; season with lemon juice, salt and pepper.

Incorporate oil in thin stream while whisking constantly.

Serve with vegetables.

How to Cook Rice

(serves 2)

1 SERVING	237 CALORIES	42g CARBOHYDRATE
3g PROTEIN	6g FAT	0.8g FIBER

Setting: HIGH

Cooking time: 15 minutes

Utensil: 12 cup (3 L) casserole

1 tbsp	(15 ml) butter
1	celery stalk, diced small
1 tbsp	(15 ml) chopped parsley
½	small onion, finely chopped
½ cup	(125 ml) long grain rice, rinsed
1 cup	(250 ml) boiling water
	salt and pepper

Place butter, celery, parsley and onion in casserole.

Mix in rice and season well. Add boiling water, cover and microwave 15 minutes.

Stir rice slightly with fork. Cover and let stand 3 minutes before serving.